Our WILD™ WORLD
SERIES

Bison

NorthWord Press
Minnetonka, Minnesota

Photography © 2001: Michael H. Francis: front and back covers, pp. 20-21, 32-33, 34, 36-37, 39; Jim Brandenburg/Minden Pictures: pp. 4, 8-9, 14-15, 24-25, 30-31, 38; Jeff Foott: pp. 5, 18, 27; Henry H. Holdsworth/Wild by Nature: pp. 6, 44; Ted Nelson/Dembinsky Photo Assoc.: p. 11; Tom & Pat Leeson: pp. 12, 16, 29; Shin Yoshino/Minden Pictures: pp. 13, 23, 35; Claudia Adams/Dembinsky Photo Assoc.: p. 41; Tim Fitzharris/Minden Pictures: pp. 42-43.

Illustrations by John F. McGee
Designed by Russell S. Kuepper
Edited by Barbara K. Harold

NorthWord Press
5900 Green Oak Drive
Minnetonka, MN 55343
1-800-328-3895

Library of Congress Cataloging-in-Publication Data

Winner, Cherie.
    Bison / Cherie Winner ; illustrations by John F. McGee.
        p. cm. -- (Our wild world series)
    ISBN 1-55971-775-0 (soft cover)
        1. Bison--Juvenile literature. [1. Bison.] I. McGee, John F., ill. II. Title. III. Series.

QL737.U53 W56 2001
599.64'3--dc21
                                        00-045561

Printed in Malaysia

10 9 8 7 6 5 4 3 2 1

Bison

Cherie Winner
Illustrations by John F. McGee

NorthWord Press
Minnetonka, Minnesota

YOU KNOW what bison look like. You've probably seen pictures of them, like the ones in this book. Maybe you've even seen some live bison.

Now imagine looking out your window and seeing bison, nothing but bison, as far as you can see. That's what North American Indians and early pioneers saw.

In the 1700s, bison ruled the prairies! They roamed from northern Canada to Texas, and from Utah to Illinois. They traveled in groups called herds. Even small herds had thousands of members. Other herds had up to 4 million bison. If all the members of a big herd had lined up one behind the other, they would have reached all the way across the country and back. And that's just one herd!

Even within a large herd, bison keep in touch with one another and move as a group.

One early pioneer thought bison had a hump like a camel, a mane like a lion, and a beard like a goat.

In the winter, bison may regularly cross icy streams in their search for food.

Scientists who study animals are called zoologists (zoe-OL-uh-jists). They estimate that by the late 1800s, fewer than 1,000 bison remained in their prairie habitat, or home. The vast herds, all those millions of bison, had been killed for their horns, hides, meat, and sometimes for sport.

The bison that survived were scattered all over North America. A few people who cared about bison brought them together to breed them. These efforts saved the bison from becoming extinct, or dying out.

Today, between 10,000 and 15,000 bison roam wild. About 350,000 bison live on ranches, no longer wild animals. They are raised for their meat.

Bison were often called buffaloes by the early settlers, and the nickname is still used today. But true buffaloes are relatives of the bison that live in Africa and Asia, the cape buffalo and the water buffalo. Only North American buffaloes are bison.

Their scientific name is *Bison bison*. They belong to the bovine (BO-vine) family, along with cattle, sheep, and goats. All of these species (SPEE-sees), or kinds, of animals have horns, feet with two toes, and a stomach with four chambers.

Bison FUNFACT:

Two of the largest wild bison herds today live in Wyoming's Yellowstone National Park and Canada's Wood Buffalo National Park.

Pages 8-9: Just after dawn and before sunset are good times for bison to feed.

Bison are one of the biggest members of their family. In fact, they are the largest land animal in North America. They are bigger than elk, bigger than moose, bigger even than the fearsome grizzly bear.

Indians had much love and respect for this huge animal that provided them with many things. They ate bison meat, made clothes and tepees from the hides, and made tools from the bones. In honor of the mighty bison, many Indian tribes made good luck drawings on rocks and cave walls called pictographs (PIK-toe-grafs) and petroglyphs (PEH-troe-glifs).

Male bison are called bulls. They may stand up to 7 feet (2.1 meters) high at the shoulder. They are 10 to 12 feet (3 to 3.6 meters) long from the tip of their nose to their rump, and they weigh up to 1 ton (2,000 pounds, or 909 kilograms). That's bigger than some sports cars!

Female bison are called cows. They are a bit smaller than bulls, standing about 5 feet (1.5 meters) tall at the shoulder. They measure 7 to 8 feet (2.1 to 2.4 meters) long, and they weigh about 800 pounds (364 kilograms).

Both bulls and cows have "beards." They usually grow longer with age,
but scientists aren't sure of their function.

Bison are not only big, they have dangerous weapons. Both cows and bulls have two black horns that grow out of the skull above the eyes. They first grow out to the side and then curve upward and inward. The tips are usually very sharp. Horns grow throughout the bison's lifetime. They are never shed, or dropped off.

Horns are made of the same material as human fingernails, but they are much thicker and stronger than fingernails. There is a core of bone inside each horn near the head.

The bison has a flat face and short snout, or muzzle. Its horns may be as wide as 2 feet (61 centimeters) from tip to tip.

Bison use their horns in several ways. Sometimes two bison "lock horns" and push each other back and forth, in a kind of shoving match to see which one is stronger. At other times a bison sweeps its head back and forth, using its horns to slash at the belly of its opponent.

If a predator, or enemy, such as a grizzly bear attacks a bison, the bison might slash it. Or the bison might charge at the predator with its head down so its horns can gore, or stab, the attacker. Bison are fierce fighters. Usually, it takes two or more predators working together to kill an adult bison. If some of them attack from the front while others attack from the rear, they might bring down the bison.

Some people say bison seem to be wearing pants, or "pantaloons," because of the shaggy, long hair on their front legs. These bison are shedding their coats.

When herd members are startled or frightened they can suddenly take off in a sprint, almost as fast as a horse.

But in order to attack a bison, predators have to catch up with it first. And that isn't easy, because bison are very good runners.

Even though their legs look short, their top speed is about 35 miles (56 kilometers) per hour. And they can keep going at that speed for more than an hour.

Early hunters quickly learned that their horses could run faster than bison over a short distance, but they could not keep running for as long. If the hunters didn't catch up to a bison within a half-mile (0.8 kilometer) or so, they never would.

Bison have a large hump over their shoulders that makes them look clumsy and slow. In fact, the hump helps them run. Inside the hump is a strong muscle that holds up the bison's huge head. It also helps the front legs reach out farther, for a longer stride.

A bison coat is unique. It has long, shaggy hair on the head, legs, and front part of the body, but very short hair on the back part. It looks as if the animal got a haircut that started at the back end and stopped in the middle! Bison also have a thick, brown beard of hair hanging from their chin.

The coat is thickest in fall and winter, to protect the bison from freezing temperatures and icy winds. The warm coat was often used as a blanket by settlers and Indians.

In spring, as the weather becomes warmer, bison shed their heavy winter coats. They look scruffy with big patches of loose hair hanging from their sides. Losing their fur makes bison itch. And to make things worse, mosquitoes seem to arrive at about the same time.

This bison head is so shaggy, you can barely see the horns. But the hump on its back is very clear.

Bison use their tails like whips to shoo the insects away, but they still get bitten, and that makes them itch even more. Imagine having dozens of mosquito bites all over you, and no hands to scratch them!

But bison are not completely helpless when they itch. They scratch themselves by rubbing against any large, sturdy object, called a head rub. It might be a tree, a big rock, or even a building. But on the prairies, or plains, head rubs aren't very common. When a good one is found it is used by many bison. In fact, they may rub so hard, they scrape the bark off trees and knock down fence posts.

In Kansas in the 1800s, people tried putting sharp spikes into telegraph poles so bison would stop rubbing on the poles. But the plan backfired. Bison loved them! The spikes made great back-scratchers.

Another way bison can scratch themselves is by rolling in a wallow. This is a bowl-shaped depression in the ground. Most wallows are 8 to 10 feet (2.4 to 3 meters) across and about 1 foot (30.5 centimeters) deep. Some are much larger. Bison make a wallow by digging up the dirt with their horns, then lying down and rolling and kicking. They stir up a lot of dust.

For a bison on the prairie in the hot summer sun, a dust bath is like a natural bug repellent.

And if the wallow is wet, such as after a big rain, the bison come out of it covered with mud. They look like a complete mess, but the layer of mud prevents insects from biting them.

Once a wallow is made, many bison use it. Some wallows are visited by bison for many years, growing larger over time as more and more bison find them. All across the plains, large wallows could still be seen decades after bison had disappeared from the region.

Wallows are one sign that bison have been in an area. Other signs are their droppings, or scat, and their tracks. Fresh bison droppings are round, flat, and gooey. They look like a mushy Frisbee lying on the ground. After they dry in the prairie sun, they don't smell too bad. And that's good, because Indians and pioneers burned these "buffalo chips" to heat their homes and cook their food.

The track left by a bison's foot, or hoof, looks like two fat bananas facing each other. Each side of the track is made by one of two toes. The whole hoofprint is round and measures about 5 inches (12.7 centimeters) across.

At one time, people thought Indians and pioneers built their roads to follow bison paths. We now know that the herds did not usually make trails. They spread out and covered a wide area as they traveled.

Occasionally the bison did stay on a narrow path where they crushed the grass as they walked, and formed a "buffalo road." But these paths usually didn't go straight. Instead, the bison zig-zagged their way across the plains. And that wouldn't make a very good road!

Bison
FUNFACT:

The skin on a bison's neck and head may be up to 1 inch (2.54 centimeters) thick. Indians made shields of this tough skin.

A herd may spend several hours each day eating.
Because their bodies are so large they need lots of food for energy.

In their wandering, bison usually do not go to the same places every year. Even if they do, they usually take different routes than they have used before.

Bison move around so much to find food. They are called herbivores (HERB-uh-vorz) because they eat only plants, mostly grass. On the plains it may look as if the grass never ends. So why would bison have to go looking for more food? If bison lived alone, they wouldn't have to travel as much. But they live in herds. And when thousands of bison come to an area, they quickly eat and trample the grass. Then they have to move on, to find more food.

The whole herd may move 10 to 15 miles (16 to 24 kilometers) in a day. In pioneer times a herd would travel hundreds of miles in one year. Today, with fences and towns blocking their way, bison can't go nearly as far as they once did. But they still roam.

During their travels, bison don't follow a pattern. They don't move north in the spring and south in the fall as many birds and other animals do, for example.

Bison just wander. Sometimes they follow the scent (SENT), or odor, of fresh grass. Sometimes they go where they found good food once before. And sometimes they keep moving until they happen to find a new source of food.

A herd could be just about anywhere at any season. Even the Indians, who knew bison well and depended on them for almost everything, rarely knew exactly where they would be.

When bison find an area with fresh grass, they stay for a few days. Eating grass and other vegetation is called grazing. If the weather is very hot, bison graze during the cooler times at dawn and dusk, and sometimes even at night. If the weather is not hot, they might graze through the afternoon as well. Once or twice a day they go to the nearest stream or pond to take a long drink. Then they return to the grazing area.

Bison
FUNFACT:

From 1913 to 1938 the U.S. minted over 1.2 billion nickels with a bison on one side. They are rare today. Bison are also found on stamps in many countries, including the U.S., Canada, Germany, and Russia.

Wading in streams or ponds is a good way to cool off.

Sometimes herd members move close together as they travel across the prairie. At other times they stay farther apart.

Bison are ruminants (ROO-mih-nunts), which means their stomach has four chambers. They chew their food several times to get all the nourishment they can from it. Bison have no upper front teeth, so when they grab a mouthful of grass, they snip it off with their sharp side teeth. Then they grind it up with their large back teeth, called molars. When they swallow it, the food enters a large chamber of the stomach where bacteria begin digestion.

Bison may graze for an hour or more at a time. Then they find a comfortable spot where they can lie down and rest. They bring up a wad of grass they swallowed earlier, called their cud, and chew it again. They swallow that mouthful, bring up another wad, and chew some more. Finally the meal is finished. It then passes to other chambers of the stomach, where digestion continues.

Bison
FUNFACT:

Birds sometimes line their nests with hair that bison have shed. It may be as long as 24 inches (61 centimeters) if it comes from the bison's head.

A group of grazing bison looks very peaceful. As some of them graze, others rest in the shade, chewing their cud. But bison are always alert for danger to the herd.

Bison don't see very well, but they have good hearing and a sharp sense of smell. When they sense danger, their ears prick up and their tail lifts. They also may make grunting and snorting noises to signal other members of the herd.

Sometimes, bison ignore a passing intruder such as a wolf or mountain lion. Other times, if the intruder seems ready to attack, they will challenge it. The bison paw the ground with their front hooves. They move closer, lowering their heads so their horns point forward. This warning is often all it takes to make the intruder back down and leave the area. But bison will fight if necesary, to protect themselves and the herd.

Even while grazing, bison are always alert to any danger that may be nearby.

If bison are startled by a sudden danger such as fire or a loud storm, they often stampede (stam-PEED). In a stampede, the whole herd races off at a full gallop. They may run for miles, not even stopping to see whether they are still in danger.

This behavior sometimes made bison easier to hunt. Indians would surprise groups of bison to make them run toward a cliff called a "buffalo jump." The stampeding bison would be running so fast that by the time they saw the cliff, they couldn't stop. Over they went, falling to their death on the rocks below. The Indians then took the bison meat and hides for their families.

If a danger is not sudden enough to make bison stampede, they move away from it more slowly. The leader of the group, usually an old cow, decides when the group should move on. She walks or trots away from the danger, and the rest of the group follows her. They keep going until she decides it is safe to stop.

Bison don't need shade to be comfortable when they rest
and chew their cud. They often just lie down near more food.

A herd is made of several smaller groups, or bands. Each band has from three to fifty members. As a herd spreads out to graze, each band stays together, but they leave space between one band and the next.

Each band includes females of all ages, their babies, or calves, and their offspring from previous years. Young bulls may stay in the band until they are four years old. Then they travel and eat on their own or with other bulls in a separate bachelor (BACH-ler) group.

Bison
FUNFACT:

From a distance, a stampeding herd sounds like thunder or a big waterfall. Some people say the ground even shakes like an earthquake.

Bison are social animals. They usually prefer to gather in groups.
But on the wide-open prairie they may wander away from the herd.

During the rut, competing bulls slowly approach each other, lower their heads, and raise their tails. Then they charge at full speed again and again until one gives up.

In late summer the breeding season, or rut, begins. Bulls start visiting bands of cows. They look for mates and try to keep other bulls away.

The bulls make a deep, loud, roaring sound called a bellow (BEL-oh), to warn other bulls to leave. They stand sideways to each other, to show how big they are. They lock horns and try to shove each other out of the way. Sometimes they fight, cutting and poking each other with their sharp horns.

Bulls also show off in the wallows. The biggest, strongest bull rolls in a wallow first, showing by his kicks and rolls how tough he is. After he leaves, all the other bulls take a turn in the wallow as the cows watch.

Sometimes bulls are so busy with these battles that they don't eat much, so they lose weight. They may also become wounded, but there is a reward. The bull that wins the rutting contests will mate with several cows. Bulls that lose these challenges probably won't mate at all that year.

The winning bull follows his group of cows for several days or weeks. He knows when a cow is ready to mate by sniffing her urine. As he sniffs, he lifts his upper lip. That lets the scent enter a special organ, called the Jacobson's organ, in the roof of his mouth. This organ is very sensitive to the chemicals in the female's urine that tell the bull she is ready to mate.

After the bull has mated with all the cows in his group, he and the cows separate again. The females go back to their band. The males go back to the bachelor group, where they can heal the wounds they received during the rut.

All of the bison must prepare for the coming winter. They must store fat to help them get through the cold months.

Bison fur is thick and repels water. It may look soft, but it actually feels rough. A bison tongue is very sensitive in choosing good grasses to eat.

Not even early snowstorms stop bison from finding
the precious food that will help them stay strong until spring.

If they can eat enough before winter comes, and if the snow isn't too deep, bison survive winter very well. They may seek shelter among trees or in the hills. Their thick coat helps them stay warm. To reach grass under the snow, they use their broad snouts to sweep aside the snow.

Icy winds that seem harsh to us actually help bison by blowing snow off the ground, so the grass is easier to see. Deep snow makes food harder to find, and it makes travel more difficult. Bison can't move very fast if they have to wade through snow up to their bellies.

Bison
FUNFACT:

At the start of winter, bison have a layer of fat nearly 2 inches (5.1 centimeters) thick on their back. By spring the fat is gone.

A bison's coat acts like a protective blanket.
The cold doesn't get in, and the bison's warm body heat doesn't get out.

Calves usually nurse for about 6 months. Mother's milk is high in protein and fat, which gives the calf lots of energy.

But even the most severe winter eventually comes to an end. The snow melts, the days grow longer and warmer, and the grass grows tall. This is the world that greets bison calves, which are born sometime between April and June. Each cow usually has one calf. Twins are very rare.

A newborn bison looks different from its parents. Its fur is reddish and it does not have a shoulder hump. It weighs between 30 and 70 pounds (13.6 to 31.8 kilograms) and is quite strong. Within a half-hour it can stand up. It begins to nurse, or drink its mother's rich milk. In a few days it is able to keep up with its mother and play with other calves.

A calf stays close to its mother for about 1 year. She protects it and teaches it many things to help it survive.

Bison mothers probably recognize their own calves by their smell and the sound of their cry, called a bleat (BLEET). But calves don't seem to recognize their own mother. If a cow and calf become separated, the calf will follow any large animal it sees, including another bison, a horse, or even a person.

This calf has a lot of catching up to do
if it is going to grow as large as its mother.

Crossing a stream or river in a group may help protect
each bison against the hidden current.

The first few months of a bison's life are very dangerous. If a calf wanders away from its mother and the rest of its band, it may become a meal for predators such as wolves and grizzly bears. Nearby bulls sometimes help calves by standing guard over them and scaring away predators.

Calves also face danger when their band crosses a river. Adults are good swimmers and don't fear the water. But a young calf may be lost if the current is swift.

A calf that escapes these dangers grows quickly. In September its shoulder hump begins to develop, its coat starts to turn dark brown, and little bumps appear on its head where horns are beginning to grow. It still nurses, but it also eats grass and sometimes other plants, as the adults do.

One of this calf's horns is starting to appear just above its eye, and its coat will soon begin to darken. These are sure signs that it is healthy and growing.

During the winter the calves huddle with their mothers and other adults, learning how to stay warm and find food.

When spring arrives, the calves are called yearlings. They are like teenagers. They have grown a lot, now weighing about 350 pounds (158 kilograms). They spend more time on their own, grazing and playing with other yearlings. Their mothers have given birth to new calves, which need lots of attention and care.

The young bison continue to grow for three or four more years, until they become adults. Then the males go off on their own, or join other young bulls in a bachelor group. The females usually stay in their mother's band.

They will roam the plains, find mates, and raise calves of their own. And the herds will grow larger and larger. Maybe one day, they will again reach as far as the eye can see.

Bison
FUNFACT:

In the early 1800s, there were at least 30 million and maybe as many as 200 million bison in North America.

Internet Sites

You can find out more interesting information about bison and lots of other wildlife by visiting these web sites.

www.animal.discovery.com	Discovery Channel Online
www.enchantedlearning.com	Disney Online
www.pbs.org/wnet/nature/buffalo	Public Broadcast Service (PBS)
www.kidsplanet.org	Defenders of Wildlife
www.nationalgeographic.com/kids	National Geographic Society
www.nwf.org/kids	National Wildlife Federation
www.tnc.org	The Nature Conservancy
www.worldwildlife.org	World Wildlife Fund

Index

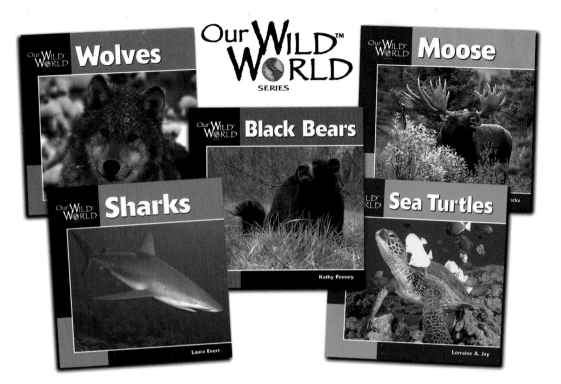

Titles available in the Our Wild World Series:

BISON
ISBN 1-55971-775-0

BLACK BEARS
ISBN 1-55971-742-4

DOLPHINS
ISBN 1-55971-776-9

EAGLES
ISBN 1-55971-777-7

MANATEES
ISBN 1-55971-778-5

MOOSE
ISBN 1-55971-744-0

SEA TURTLES
ISBN 1-55971-746-7

SHARKS
ISBN 1-55971-779-3

WHALES
ISBN 1-55971-780-7

WHITETAIL DEER
ISBN 1-55971-743-2

WOLVES
ISBN 1-55971-748-3

See your nearest bookseller or order by phone 1-800-328-3895

NORTHWORD PRESS
Minnetonka, Minnesota